Dating Someone With ADHD

The Ultimate Guide On How To Date Someone With ADHD
And
Thrive

Stephanie Mike

Table of Contents

Chapter 1

Definition and Types of ADHD

One of the most prevalent and extensively researched neurodevelopmental diseases in children is ADHD (Attention Deficit Hyperactivity Disorder). "Neuro" denotes nerves. Researchers discovered abnormalities in the brains, neural networks, and neurotransmitters of ADHD individuals. ADHD is a chronic brain illness that causes executive dysfunction, which reduces a person's ability to manage their emotions, thoughts, and actions. Individuals with ADHD struggle to:

> ***Manage their behavior.***
> ***Pay attention.***
> ***Keep things organized.***
> ***Concentrate.***
> ***Follow the instructions.***
> ***Sitting still.***
> ***Control their emotions.***

Children are routinely diagnosed throughout their childhood, and the sickness often lasts until adulthood. Fortunately, there are excellent therapies available. ADHD, if left untreated, can have serious, lifelong effects.

According to research, around 11% of U.S. Kids, between 2 to 17 years of age, have been diagnosed with ADHD. Globally, 7.2% of kids have been diagnosed with ADHD. Boys and children classified as male at birth are diagnosed with ADHD more than twice as commonly as girls and children assigned female at birth. However, this does not mean that more boys and children with AMAB have ADHD. It simply means that they are more likely to exhibit hyperactive-like symptoms and hence simpler to diagnose.

Types of ADHD

ADHD expresses itself in four distinct ways. One of four approaches is used by the providers to diagnose the illness based on the child's symptoms.

Inattentive presentation

Kids with this presentation have inattentive ADHD. Previously, doctors referred to it as attention deficit disorder (ADD). Children with inattentive presentation struggle to focus, organize, and stay on task, and they demonstrate fewer hyperactivity/impulsivity symptoms.

> - *Having difficulties organizing duties and activities.*
> - *Avoiding or detesting mental labor-intensive activities.*
> - *Continue losing things.*
> - *Easily distracted by external stimuli.*
> - *Difficulty paying attention to details or making careless mistakes.*
> - *Issues keep focused on duties and activities.*
> - *Difficulties listening, daydreaming, or appearing distracted.*
> - *Having trouble following directions and/or finishing tasks.*

Dynamic and impulsive.

Children with this presentation demonstrate hyperactivity and impulsivity, as well as less evident difficulty with concentration. Hyperactivity indicates that they fidget, cannot sit still, have a lot of energy, and are overly chatty. Impulsivity suggests a tendency to interrupt others and act without first considering the consequences. This is the least common kind, which typically affects younger children.

> - *Talking too much.*
> - *Answering queries before they are completely finished.*
> - *They frequently have trouble waiting their turn.*
> - *Frequently disrupting or invading other people's conversations or games.*
> - *Wriggling, tapping feet or hands, or fidgeting constantly.*
> - *Leaving their seat when they are expected to stay seated.*
> - *When it's not proper, running or climbing.*
> - *Difficulty playing or completing leisure activities quietly.*
> - *Always appears "on the move" or "powered by a motor."*

Combined presentation

Children with this presentation demonstrate at least six symptoms from each of the other categories. Symptoms of inattention and hyperactivity-impulsivity emerge simultaneously. This type is most commonly connected with ADHD. Approximately 70% of cases fall into this category.

Unspecified presentation

In many cases, symptoms may be so severe that children plainly demonstrate dysfunction yet may not fulfill the official symptom criteria for an ADHD diagnosis. In such cases, physicians diagnose "unspecified ADHD.

ADD & ADHD

Providers used to refer to the inattentive presenting type of ADHD as "attention-deficit disorder" (ADD). The American Psychiatric Association officially changed its name in 1994. Whether or not hyperactive symptoms are present, all forms of ADHD are now referred to as "attention-deficit/hyperactivity disorder. As previously said, physicians diagnose the different types depending on their symptoms.

Although the name was changed decades ago, many people still refer to it as attention deficit disorder (ADD). ADD and ADHD vary in that ADD does not exhibit indicators of hyperactivity or impulsivity.

Causes of ADHD

Scientists uncovered anomalies in the brain structure and function of ADHD patients. The area of your brain located behind your forehead is called the frontal lobe. The frontal lobe is in charge of organizing, focusing, making choices, and regulating behavior with words. Researchers refer to this type of behavior as focused attention. People with ADHD experience slower brain maturation than neurotypical people.

People utilize focused attention to suspend automatic attention, a second type of attention that is especially effective in ADHD patients. However, concentrated attention takes a great amount of effort and is difficult to implement. People with ADHD have poor focused attention skills. Automatic attention is the kind of attention you use when doing something interesting or engaging. When doing something boring or dull, you use directed focus. For example, in childhood, tiresome, repeated tasks.

Nerve cells, or neurons, carry impulses throughout the brain. These messages travel through your brain in groups of neurons known as networks. Scientists refer to the brain's automatic attention network as the default mode. The task-positive mode, also referred to as the executive network, is your brain's directed attention network. Researchers uncovered major networks that work differently in ADHD individuals. ADHD involves neurotransmitters, which are molecules that aid in the passage of information from one nerve cell to another.

Despite the fact that these brain changes have been detected, experts are still unaware of the specific cause and how they contribute to ADHD symptoms. However, current evidence suggests that genetics plays a crucial role. ADHD typically runs in families; a child with ADHD has a one-in-four chance of having a parent with the condition. Other variables and reasons that could contribute to ADHD include:

- *Brain anatomy.*
- *Using substances while pregnant.*
- *Premature birth.*
- *Low birth weight.*
- *Lead exposure.*

The following are not the causes of ADHD.

- *Too much time staring at screens.*
- *Poor parenting.*
- *Poverty is an example of a social and environmental issue.*
- *Allergies.*
- *Immunizations.*

Without treatment, ADHD can have a number of long-term implications. These challenges may include:

- ➤ *Substance use disorder.*
- ➤ *Risky and impulsive behavior.*
- ➤ *Uncertainty regarding employment.*
- ➤ *Accidents and injuries happen regularly while driving.*
- ➤ *Problems with relationships and other social interactions.*
- ➤ *Academic underachievement.*
- ➤ *Low self-esteem.*
- ➤ *Depression and anxiety.*
- ➤ *Eating disorders.*
- ➤ *Sleep troubles.*

Diagnosis And Tests

The American Academy of Pediatrics has developed a set of guidelines that can be utilized by the child's pediatrician or another professional to determine whether the child has ADHD. The suggestions are geared mostly toward children aged four to seventeen. ADHD is difficult to diagnose in children under the age of four because it changes so quickly, and many children at this age are naturally hyperactive or inattentive.

It may also be more difficult to diagnose ADHD in kids who are also suffering from despair or anxiety. There is no ADHD test to help diagnose the disorder. To help identify a diagnosis, the child's provider will go through several processes and gather a considerable amount of information. The critical component is that several people observe the behaviors associated with ADHD in a variety of situations, including school and home. Several people will participate in reviewing the child's behavior, including:

- ➤ *The parent*
- ➤ *The child*
- ➤ *Children's healthcare provider*
- ➤ *Teachers and other individuals who work with them*

Based on the information provided, the child's caregiver will assess how the child's behavior compares to that of other children his or her age. They will observe the child's symptoms and use DSM-5-TR criteria to help diagnose ADHD. The DSM-5-TR states that:

> ➢ *The individual's symptoms must seriously impair their capacity to do daily activities.*
> ➢ *Their symptoms must have started before they turned twelve.*
> ➢ *For at least half a year, they've exhibited symptoms.*
> ➢ *The individual's symptoms must manifest in at least two settings, such as home, school, and/or social contacts, and create disruption.*
> ➢ *The child's provider must confirm the presence or absence of six or more symptoms.*

After assessing the child's symptoms, they can make a diagnosis and identify the type of ADHD. A full assessment of behavior is required, rather than just neuropsychological attention testing, because many smart children can perform well in school despite exhibiting inattentive symptoms.

How ADHD Affects Relationships

While the disorientation, disorganization, and impulsivity of attention deficit hyperactivity disorder (ADHD or ADD) can cause problems in many facets of adult life, these symptoms can be especially damaging to your closest relationships. This is especially true if the ADHD symptoms have never been properly recognized or treated.

If you are in a relationship with someone who has ADHD, you may feel lonely, unappreciated, or undervalued. You are tired of doing everything on your own and being the lone responsible party in the relationship. You do not believe you can rely on your partner. They never seem to meet their promises, so you must constantly issue reminders and requests, or do things yourself. Sometimes it appears like your significant other does not care.

It's simple to see how both sides' feelings could contribute to a negative cycle in the relationship. The partner without ADHD gets more and more irritated, criticizes, and nags, while the partner with ADHD feels misinterpreted and gets defensive, withdrawing. Ultimately, no one is satisfied. Understanding the impact ADHD has on your relationship will help you pick more positive and constructive ways to respond to situations and communicate with one another. With these strategies, you may expand your knowledge and strengthen your connection.

Understanding how ADHD affects your relationship is the first step toward altering it. Once you've determined how ADHD symptoms are hurting your relationship interactions, you can discover more effective ways to respond. This requires understanding how to respond to adversities in ways that both inspire and thrill your partner.

The better you understand ADHD and its symptoms, the easier it will be to see how it affects your relationship. You may notice a light bulb turn on. Many of your relationship issues are now fixed! Remembering that the ADHD brain is hardwired differently than the non-ADHD brain can assist the non-ADHD partner in dealing with symptoms more effectively. Consider how your nagging and criticism impact your spouse's emotions. Don't dismiss or disregard your partner's concerns because you don't like how they bring them up or respond to you.

Chapter 2

The Early Stages of Dating

Dating with ADHD can be difficult because people with ADHD are frequently fondly referred to as autistic advocates. That's not because we're unchangeable, but because our behaviors are frequently misunderstood, our legitimate differences are rarely accommodated, and our abilities and talents aren't always acknowledged or valued.

There are far too many preconceptions regarding ADHD to count, and when people hear the phrase, they typically see a child rather than an adult. If they do imagine an adult, some see us as energizer bunnies rushing around the room or always zoning out in a trance-like state. That's a problem because when these are the pictures that come to mind, it can be difficult for them to see us as whole persons and prospective romantic partners. It's a shame because we deserve love and affection, and we have so much to offer in return.

So, to give you a crash lesson on what it's truly like to date with ADHD, here's what I wish everyone understood about how we approach dating:

Lateness
No matter how hard we try, time management remains a challenge for many ADHDers, according to 2019 research on how ADHDers perceive time. That's a problem when you have a date and need to appear on time. Our complicated relationship with timeliness may cause a lot of friction in relationships because being late is typically interpreted as disrespectful or an indication that someone does not value your time. However, this is rarely the case for those with ADHD. Being late does not imply that I do not care. Honestly, the reason we're late is mainly due to us forgetting about our schedule and becoming entirely immersed in another task, despite the fact that we have hundreds of reminder applications on our phones and sticky notes all over our homes.

Rejection

Rejection-sensitive dysphoria (RSD) occurs when you suffer intense emotional discomfort as a result of a failure or feeling rejected. Though it is not an official diagnostic or medical term, this behavior is frequently mentioned in relation to ADHD, and it came up constantly when I spoke with ADHDers about their dating experiences. RSD is extremely personal and unique to each ADHDer, but it is critical to have open, judgment-free conversations about what triggers emotions of rejection and how to move through them in any relationship.

Forgetfulness

How much we remember about other people is typically regarded as a barometer for how much we care, therefore ADHD-related forgetting is sometimes misinterpreted as an indication that we aren't interested in or appreciate someone. Just because I forget something does not mean I don't care. If an ADHDer forgets something, it could be because they are overloaded or overly focused on something else.

Eye Contact

For the most part, paying active attention entails maintaining persistent eye contact, but in multiple talks with ADHDers, many of them believe it is easier to pay attention when they do not make eye contact and instead glance away and fidget. This is especially true for those of us who are also autistic. According to some studies, people with ADHD frequently exhibit indicators of autism. So not glancing at a date doesn't necessarily imply that we're not interested. If you're dating someone with ADHD, bear in mind that gazing away from them may relieve some of their stress.

Interruption

Part of the ADHD experience is feeling as if we could explode if we are really excited about a topic and are unable to discuss it immediately. That may cause us to continually interrupt you, which is extremely typical among younger ADHDers, according to a 2000 study on communication and children with ADHD. These interruptions can also indicate that we are extremely nervous, rather than being disrespectful. I can become overly verbose and fixated on a single issue. It's my way of demonstrating that I care. So being more understanding and polite while speaking with an ADHDer might go a long way.

Inattentiveness
Attention deficiencies are such an important element of ADHD that they are mentioned in the name, but some people still take our inattention personally, assuming that it is a choice and reflects a lack of interest. We care even when we are not paying attention. So, if you're dating an ADHDer, remember that a lack of attention does not always imply a lack of concern.

Overshare
ADHD may cause some of us to open up too quickly and disclose too much. We may tell you an embarrassing anecdote to make you laugh, or we may deconstruct deep family drama in front of you because we need to get something off our chest. There are several reasons why this can happen to some of us, as I've found from speaking with hundreds of ADHDers in my advocacy work. Sometimes it's because we need to fill the silence, we want to connect with you, we don't know how much information you really need, or our impulsivity has taken over. So, if our stories are a little too much for you, we assure you that we are not intentionally making you uncomfortable.

Inconsistent
Some people with ADHD have deficiencies in executive function, which helps us regulate our emotions, motivate ourselves, accomplish activities, and prioritize, according to a 2010 study on adults with ADHD and a 2019 study on children with ADHD. So, when it comes to dating, I sometimes can't do things due to burnout. Many people do not grasp this. However, this does not imply that we will never be able to do things with you or contribute to the relationship. It simply indicates that we may need to do tasks at our own pace. Sometimes I can't clean anything for two weeks, but then I'll thoroughly clean the entire house.

Signals

When it comes to dating, ADHDers frequently admire and even rely on directness. When you aren't completely honest with us, we may overlook or misinterpret signs when you try to flirt with us. That could be because we are easily distracted by all of the sensory stimulation around us, we process information more slowly, and we are so focused on our words and their exact meaning that we miss the context of the encounter and any other signals you are sending. Even if we genuinely like you, your flexing, leaning forward, or sending "good morning" texts may not register as flirting in our brains, and we may not demonstrate that our feelings are reciprocated. I couldn't read signals if my life depended on them. Tell me straight up.

If you've noticed someone you know or feel may have ADHD, being direct can help you communicate more clearly, especially if they're also autistic. They may not understand your subtle body language and charming flirtations, but inviting them on a date will.

Excitement and Confusion

According to a 2018 study, ADHD brains frequently crave novelty and become absorbed in the delightful exhilaration of new experiences. When it comes to dating, we can confuse exhilaration with romantic impulses. To help them find out what they truly feel for someone, take things slowly so they can see if it's love or hyper fixation. If you slow down a little, we, and maybe even you, will have more time to evaluate our feelings and emotions before investing in a relationship.

Patience

Patience is essential when dealing with some ADHDers. We don't always have the stamina to respond to messages promptly, so we discuss how online dating differs for ADHDers. And, yes, we might become distracted from time to time. We would welcome patience in all aspects of our connection. Love and patience allow us plenty of room to learn, adapt, and grow.

Identity

Many people think of ADHD as a transient experience, although it can be a significant part of an ADHDer's life. ADHD is an integral part of who I am as a person. That includes understanding and honoring their differences, recognizing ADHD's role in their life, and working with them to create a truly compatible and loving relationship.

Chapter 3

Communication Strategies

For every relationship to succeed, communication is crucial. Sometimes, though, meaningful communication isn't simple. You might have distinct communication styles, or you might be prone to conflicts. Typically, couples can work past those challenges and discover ways to connect.

However, another communication challenge can occur when your partner has a disorder like ADHD. It doesn't mean healthy communication is impossible. But, you might have to alter your efforts and find different ways to communicate yourself and hear what your partner is truly saying. With that in mind, let's look at a few ways you are able to more effectively communicate with your ADHD partner.

Don't judge
The most crucial thing you can do to open up the doors of communication is not to judge or criticize your partner for their problem. They are most likely as angry about it as you are.

We don't pick their behavior, and they aren't attempting to be "difficult" on purpose. Chances are, your spouse has been suffering with symptoms since childhood. Instead of attempting to persuade someone to change, learn to appreciate the differences in your communication styles so that you may better work through them.

Give your partner full attention
This is essential in any relationship, but it is especially crucial when communicating with someone who has ADHD. When you and your lover are talking, concentrate on them. Do not allow other things to distract you. In fact, avoid having additional distracting things in the same space. You'll both be more likely to stay focused, and your partner may feel more at ease if they know you're listening directly to them and there's nothing else to distract their attention.

Do not let anything bother you
Everyone wishes to feel heard, understood, and respected in a
relationship. Unfortunately, you may not always feel this way with an
ADHD partner. You could believe they are too distracted to pay
attention. Alternatively, they may forget what you said, even if it was
significant.

Of course, those things will sting. But you cannot take it personally.
Your partner is not purposefully dismissing what you say or choosing
to forget vital information you have told them. You must be prepared
to see past the issue. They'll feel horrible enough about it when you
bring it to their attention, so don't hold a grudge or continue to
critique a disorder they can't manage.

Find what works for you both
There is no one proper approach for partners to communicate. What
works for one couple could be a tragedy for another. And, whether or
not they have ADHD, all couples experience difficulties and make
mistakes. This may sound intimidating, but it may also feel free. You
and your spouse are allowed to develop your own procedures and
rituals based on your individual traits. Experiment, discover, and
evolve.

Look inward
If there is a breakdown in communication in your relationship, it may
feel easier to "blame" everything on your partner. But this isn't fair to
any of you. Consider your own communicative function in the
connection and how you're developing it. There is always potential
for development, especially as you and your spouse grow and adapt
over time.

Don't simply play the blame game and think you're doing everything
correctly. Where do you struggle with communication? Where can
you improve? How can you make things simpler for yourself and
your partner?

Consult a professional

If you're still having trouble communicating with your ADHD partner, you should try seeing a therapist, either individually or as a couple. They can assist you in identifying a communication style that is appropriate for your relationship and meets both of your requirements. You may discover a lot more about your ADHD partner throughout therapy, including how tough communication can be for them. But you'll also acquire the tools essential to improve your communication as partners without leaning into frustration or uncertainty.

There are lots of couples with ADHD people that are happy, content, and healthy in their communication efforts. Don't assume your relationship is over just because you can't communicate adequately. Help is available and can make life easier for you and your companion.

Chapter 4

Benefits of Dating Someone with ADHD

When individuals talk about dating someone with ADHD, they generally focus on the difficulties that both couples endure. For example, a New York Times piece on the subject emphasizes discovering coping mechanisms and demonstrating to your partner that you are trying ways to manage the unique obstacles that couples may confront.

While these strategies might be beneficial, focusing on the negative aspects of ADHD relationships frequently overlooks the joy that comes with loving someone neurodiverse. The truth is that we have a lot to offer in our relationships, and while there may be particular obstacles, there are also unique opportunities.

Building confidence, trust, and joy in a relationship entails seeing those advantages in a positive way. While each individual and relationship is unique, here are five key characteristics to consider when dating an ADHD spouse.

Everyone with ADHD has a different and unique experience with the disorder. Furthermore, distinct subtypes of ADHD exhibit diverse symptoms and have yielded different results in investigations. This chapter provides a general overview of some of the difficulties that persons with ADHD commonly face, but it may not apply to everyone with the disease.

Creativity and Energy
The endless energy that keeps your spouse always moving can be daunting at times. However, if you understand what inspires your spouse, you can begin to channel that creative energy in novel new ways. Being open to new viewpoints and excitement can help alleviate monotony and renew the spark of excitement that is essential to any relationship.

Passion and spontaneity

In one poll of partners of people with ADHD, a "zest for life" was one of the top attributes most valued in the relationship. It's easy to see why; persons with ADHD have a tendency to live in the moment, which provides a delightful vitality that enervates any activity.

Seeing someone with ADHD can frequently result in having so many great date ideas that it's difficult to choose! It may be up to the non-ADHD partner to choose from an extensive list of options, but they will never be bored or run out of things to do together.

Open-mindedness

Part of treating ADHD is educating patients about how their minds work differently than those of the neurotypical population. As a result, neurodivergent couples can be more receptive to fresh thoughts and ideas.

Many persons with ADHD have reported feeling 'different' from others due to how they interpret and react to events. They can be more sensitive to persons with new ideas or interpretations, making them a helpful and understanding romantic partner.

Unique viewpoints

One often-overlooked characteristic of ADHD is the tendency to hyperfocus, spending hours at a time completely engrossed in a task that fascinates them. Time spent in a state of hyperfocus can occasionally pay off; partners frequently witness this firsthand when delving into their significant other's hobbies or interests. All it takes is effective communication, which is a crucial component of any relationship.

Empathy and Understanding

Anyone who has ever felt overloaded or scattered will find a sympathetic ear from their ADHD companion. When it comes to completing tasks and thriving with ADHD, a little empathy can go a long way. A good relationship based on kindness and understanding can flourish with an ADHD partner.

Developing an ADHD connection
Dating someone with ADHD presents unique obstacles, but the same can be said for any relationship. Understanding, communication, and successful treatment can help both couples achieve a truly thriving relationship that takes into consideration their unique backgrounds and experiences.

By learning about ADHD, communicating effectively, and being supportive, you may assist your partner in managing their illness and living a happy and fulfilling life. Remember to look for yourself and get help when you need it. With patience, compassion, and love, you and your partner can overcome any obstacle.

Chapter 5

Intimacy and Connection

In an ADHD relationship, excellent sex is only feasible when both people are relaxed, having fun, and able to tune out the outer world and enjoy the moment. This is challenging for adults with ADHD. How can a man who has problems with "lingering" have sex? How can a lady focus on receiving or providing pleasure if she is thinking about painting the living room or answering emails?

Intimacy is another important concern. Adults with ADHD crave excitement in all aspects of their lives, including relationships and sexual activity. As a love relationship progresses and cravings fade, someone with ADHD may lose interest in sex and pursue more intriguing activities or people. Boredom with sex is one of the reasons for higher divorce rates among ADHD-affected couples.

In some relationships, a lack of sexual intimacy suggests a power struggle. Typically, the partner without ADHD will gain more influence over shopping, finances, parenting, and everything else that happens at home. She eventually grows tired of having to "do all the labor" and complains to her spouse.

In the meantime, the ADHD partner begins to feel less like a lover and more like a child. This creates a dual problem: the partner without ADHD accumulates so much hostility that sex no longer sounds enticing, whilst the other partner's developing perception of his partner as a parent reduces his own sexual attraction. As a result, formerly expended energy on sex is now focused on hobbies and other nonsexual pursuits.

Time management is the problem in other partnerships. Perhaps one spouse is in the mood, while the other is fast asleep. Perhaps one is waiting patiently in the bedroom while the other searches the internet for the latest iPhone. Unfortunately, these couples frequently assume that they are unable to have sex due to an underlying disagreement when, in fact, they have a schedule conflict.

Whatever problems you have, the first step toward resolving them is to acknowledge that ADHD has a substantial impact on how you connect sexually. The second stage is to realize that the issue is likely to be biological rather than emotional. In other words, you love each other, but ADHD-induced poor behavior gets in the way.

The partner with ADHD needs to learn how to linger. Before attempting the skill in the bedroom, practice it in nonsexual settings such as talking with your spouse over coffee or going to a museum together. Both partners must let go of resentments and work to restore their relationship. A good therapist can help with these problems. If you're locked in the parent/child pattern I described, it's vital to start delegating responsibility for organization, finances, and so on. Romance will eventually be rekindled.

Every day, do something that physically connects you to your partner, such as holding his or her hand, cleaning her hair, or massaging his tired feet. Make sure to hug each other too. Make regular dates with one another, irrespective of how busy you are or how much time your children appear to consume. Set your alarm for 10 minutes earlier each morning and spend that time snuggling and exchanging good sentiments. Place love notes where your lover is likely to see them, such as in his shirt pocket or on the refrigerator.

Chapter 6

Conflict Resolution

Conflict may and does develop in all meaningful relationships. When someone with ADHD enters the picture, it can be a recipe for catastrophe if several critical tools are not used. The script usually goes like this: I want my guy to understand that I'm not doing it on purpose. He believes that I 'forget' to close the cabinets or 'forget' to put things away on purpose, or that I wish my partner appreciated how hard I tried. She just doesn't understand how much effort it takes for me to do things that she takes for granted.

Although all couples must negotiate problems, communicate well, and work together, ADHD puts a burden on a relationship. A lot of people with ADHD have partners who are so organized that people make fun of them for having Attention Surplus Syndrome. Over time, it appears that the opposing features that attracted the two to each other lose their attractiveness and might even become the source of conflict.

Thus, when a dispute arises, step aside and calm down. Give yourself time to examine your emotions before replying. This can prevent impulsive reactions that could worsen the issue.

Practice active listening
Avoid interrupting the other person and instead attentively listen to their point of view. Don't jump to conclusions or make assumptions. Listening without judgment or defensiveness allows you to grasp their point of view and promotes greater communication.

Break it down
If the disagreement appears overwhelming, break it down into smaller, more manageable chunks. Address each issue one at a time to prevent feeling overwhelmed and to keep his/her focus. Seek clarification.

If you are confused about something, feel free to ask for clarification. It is acceptable to seek further information to ensure that you comprehend the situation completely.

Practice empathy

Try to grasp the other person's feelings and perspectives. This may encourage a more considerate and useful approach to conflict resolution.

Use "I" statements

Use "I" expressions to express your feelings or concerns without appearing accusing. Say something like, "I feel hurt when," rather than "You always."

Seek support

Reach out to a trusted friend, family member, or therapist for emotional support and guidance during a conflict. If you are having frequent conflicts with your partner or spouse, you should seek couples therapy with an ADHD-experienced therapist.

Set boundaries

Set boundaries for conflict resolution conversations, such as taking breaks if emotions become too intense. Share these boundaries with the other person to ensure a respectful and fruitful conversation.

After the conflict has been resolved, spend some time considering what occurred and what you learned from the experience. This can benefit personal development and future conflict resolution skills.

Chapter 7

Preventing Burnout

Being in a relationship is difficult; but, being in a partnership with someone who has ADHD adds another dimension of complexity. Here are some practical methods for avoiding ADHD burnout symptoms, improving your relationship, and deepening your connection.

Understanding how ADHD affects your partnership will allow you to effectively handle ADHD relationship concerns while also reducing frustration and exhaustion. Some of the symptoms experienced by people with ADHD might have an impact on their relationships.

ADHD symptoms include inattentiveness, impulsivity, and emotional dysregulation. As a result, lack of focus and emotional dysregulation may disrupt your communication with one another. It may appear that your partner is not entirely present during a conversation, which can create dissatisfaction and exacerbate burnout.

Your partner's impulsivity and distractibility can make it difficult for them to complete the duties that you have assigned to them. This can also have an impact on money management or housework; one partner may feel obligated to take on responsibility for keeping everything running smoothly. Taking on too much responsibility might also prevent one partner from acquiring burnout as a result of excessive caregiving duties. Five tips to avoid burnout:

Communication is crucial
The first step is to incorporate communication into your daily routine as a pair. Creating mechanisms that support the individual with Attention Deficit Hyperactivity Disorder is a key step toward effective ADHD management. Systems apply to all aspects of life, including communication.

Set aside time once a week for you and your partner to talk about your family's schedule, tasks that need to be accomplished, obstacles that may hinder the tasks from being finished, and how you can both help each other. Couples who make time to speak frequently report significant differences in overall quality of life. During your weekly meeting, add what you love about your partner so that you may highlight what is working well between the two of you.

By developing a proactive strategy, you will improve communication, and self-awareness for both partners and normalize the issues that couples face. Many couples avoid discussing hard things, but this technique promotes open communication about emotions and behavior, so minimizing burnout.

Setting appropriate boundaries
It is normal for the non-ADHD partner to believe they are in charge of the majority of household tasks. They may believe that in order to ensure the family's well-being, they must handle everything, which is a recipe for tiredness, burnout, and potential interpersonal issues.

By speaking on a weekly basis and establishing boundaries for each partner's obligations, the couple can foster a collaborative dynamic that benefits both of them. Healthy limits minimize burnout and allow each partner to meet their emotional needs while maintaining realistic expectations about each other's abilities.

Practice kindness
People with ADHD frequently struggle with remaining focused, impulsive behavior, increased emotional reactivity, and task completion. It is critical for the non-ADHD spouse to understand that their ADHD partner does not want to forget to do something. It's not always about "working harder" for them.

As a result, the non-ADHD partner must practice self-compassion towards themselves. Feelings of frustration, fatigue, disappointment, and a variety of other emotions may arise. By practicing self-compassion for yourself, you may make room for those emotions, allowing you to cope with your experience and avoid burnout.

It is also crucial to be compassionate toward your ADHD partner. Recognize how they may be feeling and approach their difficulties with compassion so that you can both help one another. Compassion enables couples to have a robust and dynamic connection regardless of any underlying mental health concerns.

Practice self-care, both individually and as a pair
It is easy to become overwhelmed when you are in a relationship with someone who has ADHD. Self-care is vital for both partners to allow them to process the beauty and hardships of being in a partnership. Self-care is more than just having a manicure or a massage; it works best when it is aligned with your fundamental beliefs and honors what is most important to you.

Despite being in a committed relationship, each partner has individual interests. Making time for activities that match your fundamental values will help each of you show up as your best self, preventing burnout.

Values also lay the groundwork for relationships, albeit intentionally. Making time for activities that are consistent with these ideals helps strengthen the relationship between the spouses. With patience, love, understanding, and basic values, it is possible to overcome the challenges that ADHD may provide, thereby strengthening the couple's bond.

Relationships and life in general are challenging and can leave us feeling overwhelmed. Being in a relationship with someone who has ADHD poses distinct obstacles. Taking care of your own mental health by engaging with a therapist often is an act of self-care. Making time to speak with a mental health expert during therapy can benefit both adults in the relationship. Therapy can allow the non-ADHD partner to focus on their own well-being, which helps lessen stress and anxiety while also working through symptoms of burnout and other concerns.

Conclusion

ADHD influences relationships in various ways. Your partner may exhibit evident signs and symptoms that have a substantial influence on their professional and social lives. On the other hand, they may simply exhibit a few ADHD symptoms, resulting in minor impairment. Whether your partner seeks help and treatment can have an impact on how they communicate and manage their commitments and relationships. The following is a summary of some frequent traits of ADHD and how they could affect a relationship:

Difficulty focusing
Due to weak focus, the individual may zone out during interactions.

Forgetfulness
A person with ADHD might agree or promise to perform a given work or conduct an errand and then forget about it later. They may also commit to social plans and neglect to show up.

Poor planning and time management
The individual may leave home activities incomplete, producing more labor for their partner. They may have difficulties arranging meals, scheduling work, or being on time.

Impulsivity
An ADHDer has a tendency to interrupt or say things without thinking, which can harm the other person's feelings. Depending on the situation and kind of ADHD, impulsive actions or dangerous behaviors might have an influence on relationships.

Emotional Reactivity
ADHD can make it difficult to maintain emotional control. This can result in outbursts of wrath or irritation. In most cases, the individual is dissatisfied with the situation, not the other party.

Love Bombing
Early in a relationship, a person with ADHD may express intense, often overpowering, affection. After the novelty wears off, they may withdraw, causing uncertainty and dissatisfaction.

It's critical to realize that ADHD alters the brain's structure, chemistry, and function, resulting in numerous behavioral traits and patterns. The ensuing symptoms, like being preoccupied during talks, may leave you feeling ignored or unnoticed.

Learning more about the symptoms will help you better understand and interpret your partner's actions, as well as find effective methods to support them.

The good aspects of ADHD, as well as the ADHDer's strengths, can enhance a relationship. Learning to appreciate those characteristics in the person you're dating is one approach to deepening your relationship. Consider the incredible level of inventiveness that many ADHDers possess. Many people thrive at thinking outside the box and developing novel solutions to issues. As you grow to know somebody better, you may notice things from a different perspective.

Most ADHDers are enthusiastic, active, and empathic, with a good sense of humor. Of course, like everyone else, each ADHDer has a distinct personality, strengths, and values. Don't draw inferences about how ADHD may influence your partner. Instead, spend time learning about their perspectives and how they handle various parts of their lives.

Supporting a Partner with ADHD

Living with ADHD is not easy. What matters most is that you work as a team to resolve and prevent repeated disagreements. Here are some suggestions for how to support someone with ADHD while maintaining your own mental health and requirements.

Work on Your Communication
It is critical that you communicate with your partner about how you feel and how their behaviors affect you. Letting frustration or disappointment grow can destroy a relationship. However, delivering this information in an accusatory or critical tone may cause your spouse to shut down and become defensive.

Try using more "I feel" or "I desire" statements in your conversations. You can say, "I feel like I'm not significant when you interrupt me when I'm talking." This is a better technique than asking, "Why don't you ever listen to me when I speak?"

Remember that communication requires both parties to participate. Actively listen to your spouse as they speak, and provide a safe space for them to express their challenges and thoughts. Rather than presenting your partner's thoughts and feedback as a counter-argument immediately away, try to visualize them favorably.

Develop helpful coping strategies together
In most cases, adult ADHD is characterized by persistent inattention. This might cause problems at home, such as poor communication, failure to accomplish household responsibilities, and forgetting errands, appointments, or significant dates. You can address this by sitting down with your partner and discussing which tactics can be implemented at home to overcome these issues. Here are some examples of how an ADHDer can handle their household and relationship commitments:

- *Create a rotating menu together and streamline meal prep to lessen the mental load*
- *Assess your household budget and keep track of your financial spending utilizing an app.*
- *To ensure that you are not the only one responsible for remembering important dates and occasions, encourage your spouse to create phone reminders.*
- *Divide the jobs and make a to-do list or cleaning schedule for your house.*
- *Set up bill payment reminders or automated payments.*

While you can assist your partner in establishing organizational processes, it is critical that you avoid a parent-child dynamic. So, take a step back and sit down with your partner to discuss each other's roles. Suggest techniques, but encourage your partner to determine what works best for them and to seek further support along the way. By clarifying these expectations, you'll set up your partnership for success.

Compliment your partner
It is crucial to remember that each individual and relationship has distinct qualities, and it is beneficial to highlight these. So, take the initiative to thank and complement them. According to research, ADHD is related to decreased self-esteem and confidence in adulthood. Furthermore, it costs nothing to be supportive and appreciative.

Take note of your partner's individual qualities and abilities. Maybe they're amazing at a certain sport or brilliant at cooking. Perhaps they're the most generous and caring person you've encountered. Pointing these strengths out is a wonderful way of reminding people what they're genuinely capable of. You can also make it a point to acknowledge and thank them for what they do for you.

Encouraging Your Partner to Seek Help.

ADHD cannot be cured, although it is very treated. Medications and therapy can help a person manage their symptoms and operate better on a daily basis. An ADHD management strategy may also involve ADHD coaching and counseling.

If your partner hasn't previously sought professional aid or treatment, encourage them to do so. Don't be pushy or judgmental of their decisions and opinions. Instead, remind them of the advantages of receiving treatment. If they are hesitant or afraid about seeing a doctor, ask them why. Furthermore, you can offer to be their rock of support as they seek the assistance they require.

Remember that they can choose to seek expert treatment. The greatest method to help is to de-stigmatize the topic and provide support throughout the diagnostic or treatment process. Getting relationship or marriage treatment from a therapist or health professional who specializes in ADHD is an additional choice.

Draw Healthy Boundaries

Healthy limits are necessary in all relationships. It is critical that you understand what you are willing to compromise on and what you will not tolerate. Knowing your boundaries in a relationship is one approach to practicing self-care. This maintains the partnership functioning and encourages both partners to practice mutual respect.

Sit down and talk about your limits to establish clear expectations in the partnership. These usually involve emotional, financial, and physical boundaries. For instance, your partner will need time and space by themselves to work through a problem; you won't be handling all of the chores or paying all of the bills.

You may need to devise unique techniques to help each other meet such standards. Creating a chore plan or regimen might assist remind your partner to fulfill their portion of home tasks.

A happy and successful relationship requires commitment and patience. If both partners are prepared to learn and grow together, you can work out your differences and develop customized techniques to mitigate the effects of ADHD on your relationship. The idea is to set clear boundaries and schedule time for self-care activities. You don't want to be running on empty in any relationship, even one with ADHD.